W9-BKC-094

This book is presented to:

_____

Copyright © 2020 by Dr. Josh and Christi Straub
All rights reserved.
ISBN: 978-1-0877-3038-7
Published by B&H Publishing Group, Nashville, Tennessee

Unless otherwise noted, all Scripture quotations are taken
from the Christian Standard Bible®, Copyright © 2017
by Holman Bible Publishers. Used by permission.
Christian Standard Bible® and CSB® are federally registered
trademarks of Holman Bible Publishers.
Scriptures marked NIV are taken from the Holy Bible,
New International Version®, NIV® Copyright ©1973, 1978,
1984, 2011 by Biblica, Inc. Used by permission.
All rights reserved worldwide.
DEWEY: C232.92
SUBHD: JESUS CHRIST--NATIVITY / CHRISTMAS /
DEVOTIONAL LITERATURE
Printed in Dongguan, Guangdong, China, in June 2021
2 3 4 5 6 7 • 25 24 23 22 21

25 Days of the Christmas Story

An Advent **Family** Experience

Dr. Josh and Christi Straub

Illustrations by Jane Butler

B&H
kids

Nashville TN

Introduction

Our children love hearing stories about the day they were born. When we show them pictures of when Christi was pregnant, they ask all kinds of questions. And every time, their questions remind us of another story that happened prior to, during, or in the days following their birth.

The same is true with stories of adoption. Our family friends who adopt celebrate "Gotcha Days" and "Homecoming Days." The questions kids ask about their adoption days also lead to forgotten or untold stories.

If we don't share or write down our birth and adoption stories, important memories can easily be forgotten. This is one reason we tell as many stories as we can. It's also fun to see how each individual story contributes to the grander story of our child's place in our family: the significance of his or her name, how their siblings and relatives responded to their arrival, and more.

Celebrating the details of each individual story makes for an even more meaningful birthday each year.

That's why our family throws Jesus a birthday party on December 25. This is not just a birthday party we put together at the last minute. Instead, we prepare for it during each of the twenty-four days leading up to Christmas.

This is the heart behind *25 Days of the Christmas Story: An Advent Family Experience*. The word *advent* means "coming."

In the weeks leading up to Christmas, we want your family to take the time to remember and experience the people, places, and things related to the day Jesus came into the world as a baby.

On each day of December, we introduce a new story in chronological order of the events of Christmas. While this book is designed for families with children ages four to eight, feel free to tailor the stories, activities, and experiences to fit your family. Use as little or as much of the material as possible, depending on the time you have.

You do not have to add anything more to your day. This Advent family experience intentionally helps you talk about the Christmas story during times you already spend with your kids. For example, you could read the Bible verse and story in the morning, pray during a car ride, do the family activity after dinner, and discuss the questions at bedtime.

Whatever you do, make it your own, and have fun! Remember, this book is for your family to experience together.

Our kids grow up so quickly, and Christmases come and go. But the memories can be cherished for a lifetime. That's why we included pages in the back of the book to record answers to the Family Time Questions and memories you shared doing the Family Activity.

Our prayer is that this book serves as a keepsake—that the stories prepare your family's hearts to celebrate Jesus' coming and the memories bring you joy for years to come.

Merry Christmas!
Josh + Christi

Contents

Day 1

Isaiah

Character Trait: Hopeful

Isaiah and the Christmas Story

The name Isaiah means "Yahweh saves." Do you know what other name means "Yahweh saves"? Jesus! As a prophet of hope, Isaiah was someone who brought messages from God to His people. Nearly eight hundred years before Jesus was born, God told Isaiah that He was sending a "Chosen One," or the "Messiah," to deliver the people from their sin. *Eight hundred years.* That's a long time to wait! Isaiah was specific too. He spoke of the Messiah being born of a virgin and called Him "Wonderful Counselor" and "Prince of Peace" (Isaiah 9:6).

Isaiah also called Him "Immanuel" (Isaiah 7:14). *Immanuel* means "God with us." Jesus is God, but He temporarily left His place in heaven to become a baby on earth. Jesus grew into a man and lived among other people. Why is this important? It means Jesus understands everything we go through because He went through it too! So when you feel sad, you know that God knows what sadness feels like. More than that, He's with you when you feel sad. He's with you when you feel angry. He's with you when you feel happy. So no matter how you feel or what's going on in your life, you always have hope that *God is with you.* He is Immanuel.

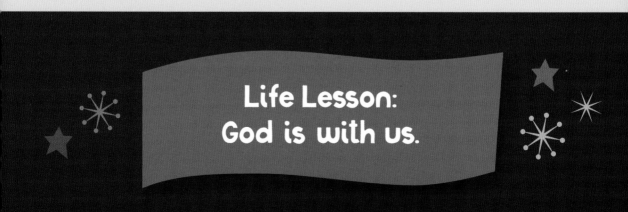

Life Lesson:
God is with us.

Family Activity

Ask everyone to draw a picture of a recent moment when they felt sad, scared, or alone. Then take turns talking about each moment as a family. After everyone shares, draw an image of Jesus beside you in the picture. Come back together and ask each family member, "The next time you feel sad, scared, or alone, how will it change the way you approach the situation if you picture Jesus beside you?" Finally, write "HOPE" across the top of the picture. Hang all the illustrations on the refrigerator as a reminder during this Christmas season that God is with us.

Family Time Question

Have you ever felt like God was with you in a particular situation? Describe that moment.

"Therefore, the Lord himself will give you a sign: See, the virgin will conceive, have a son, and name him Immanuel."
–Isaiah 7:14

Immanuel, give each of us the hope that You are "God with us" in whatever situation we may face.

David

★ Character Trait: **Faith-Filled**

David and the Christmas Story

Not only is Jesus God's Son, but He also had parents during His time on earth. Jesus' dad, Joseph, adopted Him into the family lineage of David, and His mom, Mary, was also of the bloodline of David. In case you wondered, this is David, the same shepherd boy who defeated Goliath! Can you believe it? Jesus became a long-distance grandson (twenty-eight generations) of David, fulfilling a prophecy spoken hundreds of years earlier about the coming Messiah as a descendant of David (2 Samuel 7:12–16).

People who lived when Jesus was born knew who David was. He had grown up to become a king and write the book of Psalms. But even more important, David's faith grew, and he became known as "a man after [God's] own heart" (1 Samuel 13:14).

Whenever Jesus was called "the Son of David" in the Bible, it was by people who had faith that Jesus was the promised Messiah, or the long-awaited Deliverer. They believed Jesus had the power to deliver them from suffering and illness. So when He arrived, they exploded with hope and joy.

Life Lesson:
God is my deliverer.

Family Activity

Prepare a special dessert ahead of time, but don't tell your kids! First, blindfold them. Then lead them through a list of sensory tasks. Before you begin each task, ask them if they still trust you. Grab a candle or other aromatic item and ask what it smells like. After that, lead them into the bathroom where they will wash their hands. Last, lead them into the kitchen. Ask them to open their mouths. Stick a bite of their favorite dessert inside! Then remove the blindfold.

Ask your kids what it felt like to go on that journey blindfolded. Were they scared? Did they trust you? Use this exercise to discuss putting your faith in God even when you don't know where He's leading you.

Family Time Questions

- What does it mean to put your faith in someone?

- Can you think of an example of when you put your faith in Jesus and He delivered you?

Joseph also went up from the town of Nazareth in Galilee, to Judea, to the city of David, which is called Bethlehem, because he was of the house and family line of David, to be registered along with Mary, who was engaged to him and was pregnant.–Luke 2:4–5

Lord Jesus, build our faith in You no matter what we face. Help us trust that You, the Son of David, will be our Deliverer.

Zechariah

Character Trait:
Prayerful

Zechariah and the Christmas Story

Zechariah was a priest who served in the temple and obeyed God. For a long time, Zechariah and his wife, Elizabeth, could not have children. But that did not stop Zechariah from praying for a child and believing he and Elizabeth would have one. One day, when Zechariah was an old man, an angel named Gabriel appeared to him. The angel said, "Your prayer has been heard." Zechariah was going to have a son. It was a miracle!

Read Luke 1:13-19. Notice that the angel told Zechariah to name his son John and said that John would become great in the sight of the Lord. When John grew up, he prepared the people for the coming Messiah, Jesus. Though we don't know exactly what Zechariah asked for when he prayed, this passage shows that God answered Zechariah's prayer in a much bigger way than just by giving him a baby. God used Zechariah's son to prepare the people for the coming of Jesus!

Life Lesson: Pray big prayers.

Family Activity

Gather at the table with paper and pens for everyone. Ask each family member to draw a picture of one way they can help the world around them. To generate ideas, ask, "What makes you sad? What feels heavy on your heart?" Next, ask everyone to write down a prayer to meet that need. Make it a BIG prayer that would bless others and point them to Jesus.

Remind your kids that their prayers may not be answered for years. Zechariah's part in the Christmas story shows us that God is bigger than the burdens we carry and that, sometimes, His answers will blow us away! At the end, tell everyone to attach their prayer to their bedroom door to remember to pray it often.

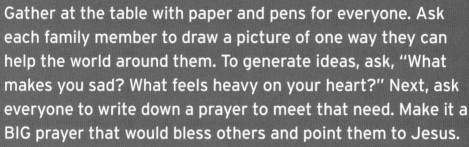

Family Time Questions

- Talk about a prayer God answered for you.

- How long did it take for Him to answer?

But the angel said to him, "Do not be afraid, Zechariah, because your prayer has been heard. Your wife Elizabeth will bear you a son, and you will name him John." –Luke 1:13

Father, teach our family to pray big prayers, especially prayers that bless others.

Elizabeth

Character Trait:
Teachable

Elizabeth and the Christmas Story

Elizabeth was Zechariah's wife and an older relative of Mary, Jesus' mother. God used Elizabeth's pregnancy as a way to provide comfort to Mary. As a woman not yet married and still a virgin, Mary was scared when Gabriel told her that she would give birth to Baby Jesus. She knew it was unacceptable to be pregnant before marriage. That's why the angel Gabriel comforted Mary by telling her that Elizabeth, her much older relative, was six months pregnant with a child she also did not expect.

The Bible says that Mary hurried to Elizabeth's house when she heard the news. We can only imagine the comfort and guidance Mary was looking for. She needed someone to talk to, someone to help her through her pregnancy. And what did Elizabeth do when Mary arrived? She welcomed her with open arms! As Mary's older relative and a woman Mary looked up to, Elizabeth invited Mary to stay with her for three months. Together, Elizabeth and Mary celebrated the miraculous baby boys God had given them.

Life Lesson:
Seek godly mentors.

Family Activity

Grab a picture frame with as many slots as you have family members. Then, as a family, talk about *mentors* and what it means to be *teachable*. A *mentor* is a godly person we can look up to and trust when we need help. Being *teachable* means having ears to listen to the wisdom mentors share. Invite everyone in the family to brainstorm a list of possible mentors. These mentors can be older family members, pastors, coaches, teachers, or neighbors. Over the next month, each family member will find or take a picture with one of the people and put it in one of the slots. Hang the picture frame in your house as a reminder of those who love and support your family.

Family Time Questions

- Name three people you know personally that you want to be like when you grow up.

- What is it about them you admire?

"And consider your relative Elizabeth—even she has conceived a son in her old age, and this is the sixth month for her who was called childless. For nothing will be impossible with God."—Luke 1:36-37

Father, help us be teachable and find godly mentors. Provide men and women who will encourage us to walk in Your ways.

23

Mary

★

Character
Trait:

Humble

Mary and the Christmas Story

Mary is the mother of Jesus. How amazing is that? Why do you think God chose her for something so important? Do you think Mary was a princess? Or maybe she was rich? Do you think she was famous?

Mary wasn't any of these things. Mary was young and poor. Many Bible teachers believe she was about fourteen years old when she became pregnant with Jesus because that was the common age for young girls to marry. Mary also lived in a tiny village of little importance. More than that, she was a virgin, which meant she couldn't have a baby yet. Young. Poor. Not famous. Unable to have a child. Does that sound like someone you might choose to be Jesus' mother? Probably not. But Mary was humble.

The Bible says that God honors those with humble hearts, people who put God first even when it might cost them something. To be humble also looks like not bragging about yourself and serving others without expecting to be praised. A humble person behaves as if only God is watching. God chose Mary, a young woman who was not very important in the eyes of the world, to be the mother of the Savior of the world. Why? Because Mary's humble heart was clear when she answered the angel Gabriel and said, "I love God. I'll do whatever He asks of me."

Life Lesson:
God looks at the heart.

Family Activity

Gather all the flashlights, electric lanterns, or small lamps you can find. Put them on the table. Turn the lights on. Discuss the differences between each one. Walk around the house and discuss how these lights differ from the floor and table lamps. Ask, "Which flashlight is everyone's favorite?" and "Is there a lamp you wouldn't use because it's ugly?" Decide on the ugliest lamp. Then read 1 Samuel 16:7 together. Discuss how no matter what a lamp looks like, the most important thing about it is the light coming from inside. In a similar way, no matter how popular, good-looking, talented, or rich a person is on the outside, God looks at the light shining in his or her heart. Mary's heart was a bright light in God's eyes!

Family Time Questions

- What is one thing you have thought about doing for another person to show God's love but haven't done yet?

- Will you do it even if no one is looking and you don't get any praise?

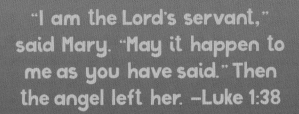

"I am the Lord's servant," said Mary. "May it happen to me as you have said." Then the angel left her. —Luke 1:38

Day 5

Father, create in us a humble and pure heart. May we, like Mary, find favor with You.

Joseph

Character
Trait:
Integrity

Joseph and the Christmas Story

Joseph was a young carpenter, engaged to Mary, when she told him she was going to have a baby. Joseph had a big decision to make. Since they were not yet married and Mary was pregnant, he knew the Jewish people would not approve and Mary would be in trouble. Because Joseph cared for Mary, he made a plan to protect her and end their engagement quietly. But then, an angel of the Lord came to Joseph in a dream. "Don't be scared to marry Mary," the angel said. "The baby is from the Holy Spirit."

God picked Joseph to become Jesus' dad on earth. How cool is that? In Jewish culture, not many men would raise a child who was not his. In spite of what others thought, Joseph was a man of *integrity*. In other words, Joseph didn't just say he believed in God; he also did what God wanted him to do. Joseph raised Jesus as his son, teaching Him to be a carpenter and loving Him with his whole heart. Joseph could have left Mary to raise Jesus on her own. But instead of doing what people around him expected, he did what God wanted him to do. As a result, Joseph had the unbelievable privilege of being Jesus' dad.

Life Lesson:
Do what is right, not what is expected.

Family Activity

Play an integrity game. Take two pieces of paper. Write "Yes" on one piece and "No" on the other. Divide the room into two sides with rope or a piece of tape, placing the "Yes" paper on one side and the "No" paper on the other.

Everyone takes turns presenting situations that test someone's integrity. For instance, you can share the following scenario: Connor accidentally breaks his sister's notebook. When she asks him about it, he says he wasn't playing with it. Invite your children to step over to the "Yes" side if they think Connor was acting with integrity and to the "No" side if they don't. Ask, "What would God want you to do?" Adjust for age.

✳ Family Time Question

- Name someone you know who often seems to do what God wants even when it's unexpected.

- Describe that person.

But after he had considered these things, an angel of the Lord appeared to him in a dream, saying, "Joseph, son of David, don't be afraid to take Mary as your wife, because what has been conceived in her is from the Holy Spirit."—Matthew 1:20

God, help us be people of integrity, doing what's right, not what's expected.

Gabriel

Character Trait:

Courageous

Gabriel and the Christmas Story

Gabriel is an angel, a messenger of God. He visited Daniel in the Old Testament to send him a prophetic message about the "Anointed One" (Daniel 9:25). He visited Zechariah in the New Testament (see Day 3) to tell him that his son, John the Baptist, would get the people ready for Jesus. Perhaps Gabriel's most famous encounter was when he visited Mary (see Day 5) to announce that her son would be "the Son of the Most High." Wow! Can you imagine? Whenever Gabriel appeared in Scripture, he delivered good news about the anticipated coming of Jesus, the Messiah.

Although people think of angels as adorable beings with wings, the Bible paints a more extraordinary picture. For example, Daniel was so scared when he saw Gabriel that he fell facedown. Zechariah, upon seeing Gabriel, was "terrified and overcome with fear" (Luke 1:12). That is because Gabriel is strong—an angel who "stands in the presence of God" (Luke 1:19). Yet he is also a creature of God's peace. Gabriel reassured each person he spoke to: "Do not be afraid." Sent by God to prepare Mary for Jesus' birth, Gabriel's message to us is also clear: In Jesus, we have nothing to fear. With God, we can be courageous.

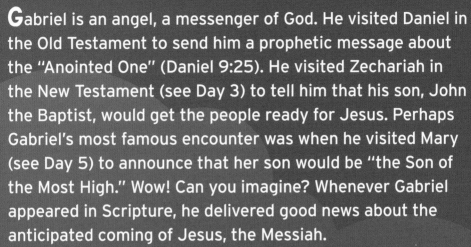

Life Lesson:
Do not be afraid.

Family Activity

Whenever Gabriel talked about the coming Messiah, he always began with "Be not afraid." Ask your children to draw a picture of something they fear. Talk about why it makes them afraid. Next, use the visual illustration of fire to represent fear. Light a candle. Then find an age-appropriate news clip of a recent wildfire to show your children how quickly fire can grow out of control. Explain how fear is like a fire. It starts small, but if you feed it, it takes over your mind.

Now invite your children to blow out the candle and repeat Gabriel's words: "Do not be afraid." Use this as a reminder when you get scared. Jesus is bigger than your fear.

Family Time Question

When you get scared, how do you calm yourself down?

The angel answered him, "I am Gabriel, who stands in the presence of God, and I was sent to speak to you and tell you this good news."—Luke 1:19

Father, help us trust You with our fears. Give us Your spirit of peace and help us be courageous.

John the Baptist

Character
Trait:
Prepared

John the Baptist and the Christmas Story

John the Baptist was the miracle baby of Zechariah and Elizabeth (see Day 3). John, like Isaiah, was a prophet. However, John lived a long time after Isaiah did. By the time John the Baptist arrived, there hadn't been a prophet in Israel for hundreds of years. So you can imagine when the Israelites learned about John, they crowded around him to hear what he said! John told people to prepare their hearts. "Look," he said as Jesus approached, "the Lamb of God, who takes away the sin of the world!" (John 1:29).

The word *advent* means "coming." The first Christmas was about the coming of Jesus. And John the Baptist announced that Jesus had come! Today, as we celebrate Christmas, we remember to prepare our hearts for the second coming of Jesus, when He will return again to the earth. Nobody knows when He will come, but we do know we can be ready. John the Baptist told the people to prepare their hearts, turn away from sin, and ask Jesus to forgive them. We can do the same today—prepare our hearts for Jesus on Christmas morning as we wait for His return.

Life Lesson: Prepare your heart.

Family Activity

Grab some straw or a manger from a nativity set and wrap it as an enticing Christmas present. Place it under your family Christmas tree in the morning but do not let your kids open it. Build anticipation throughout the day. Discuss how hard it is to wait on something.

Later that evening, invite them to open it. Was it what they expected? Use the straw to illustrate how the Israelites also waited for a gift from God: a powerful coming king. Yet Jesus arrived as a baby in a manger and almost went unnoticed, which was not what they expected! Display the straw as a reminder of Jesus' first coming and how we need to prepare our hearts for His return.

Family Time Questions

- Name one thing that has happened to you that you were not prepared for.

- In what ways can you prepare your heart for the day Jesus returns?

"And he will go before him in the spirit and power of Elijah, to turn the hearts of fathers to their children, and the disobedient to the understanding of the righteous, to make ready for the Lord a prepared people." –Luke 1:17

God, prepare our hearts for the coming Messiah. Teach us to turn from sin and seek Your forgiveness.

Day 8

Holy Spirit

Character
Trait:
Joyful

The Holy Spirit and the Christmas Story

Without the Holy Spirit, there is no Christmas story. The Holy Spirit is God. He is the Third Person of the *Trinity*—the Father, the Son, and the Holy Spirit. Not only did the Holy Spirit play a major part in the creation of the world (Genesis 1:2), but He also visited Mary to make Jesus become a baby inside of her. This miracle is known as the *incarnation*, and it's powerful to the Christian faith because it means that Jesus is both God and man—something nobody else in the history of the world can claim!

After the Holy Spirit visited Mary, He kept sprinkling joy throughout the Christmas story. When Mary arrived at Elizabeth's house (see Day 4), the baby inside Elizabeth's womb was filled with the Holy Spirit and leaped with joy. As Mary greeted her, Elizabeth was also filled with the Holy Spirit and let out a "loud cry" as she exclaimed, "Blessed are you among women, and your child will be blessed!" (Luke 1:42).

Filled with the Holy Spirit and overcome with joy, Elizabeth praised God with Mary. Not only did these women carry two baby boys who were about to change history, but they also were saved by the Messiah in Mary's womb—the baby Jesus!

Life Lesson: Be joyful.

Family Activity

Create a playlist of dance-worthy, joyful Christmas songs your kids love. Next, prepare a room for a dance party. Grab several deflated balloons. Then, to illustrate joy, ask your kids a series of questions like, "What's your favorite game to play with friends?" and "What's the happiest moment you remember from this year?" As your kids answer each question, blow a deep breath of air into a deflated balloon.

Once the balloon is full, explain how we can get so full of joy we have to let it out. This is why John the Baptist leaped in Elizabeth's womb! Let the balloon release. Watch it swirl around the room. For effect, time the release of the balloon with the beginning of the dance party.

Family Time Questions

- Talk about a time when you leaped for joy.
- What was so joyful about that moment?

Day
9

When Elizabeth heard Mary's greeting,
the baby leaped inside her, and Elizabeth
was filled with the Holy Spirit.—Luke 1:41

God, fill our hearts this
Christmas with the joy of
our salvation!

Caesar Augustus

Character
Trait:
Organized

Caesar Augustus and the Christmas Story

Caesar Augustus was the first emperor of the Roman Empire. He brought stability and organization to the Roman world. Right before the birth of Jesus, Caesar Augustus wanted to make sure everyone paid their taxes. So he took a census, gathering a list of the names of everyone living throughout the land. Because of the census, Joseph and Mary had to return to Bethlehem, where Joseph's family was from, to be counted and added to the list.

Caesar Augustus likely never knew who Jesus was. He lived 1,500 miles from where Jesus was born. Not only that, he died when Jesus was about nineteen, before Jesus became well known. Yet, because Caesar Augustus ordered the census, the prophecy that Jesus would be born in Bethlehem was fulfilled (Micah 5:2). Even 600 years before Caesar Augustus lived, God had a plan to use him. Although Caesar Augustus didn't know it at the time, his leadership provided the stability and organization of roads throughout the Roman Empire to help Christianity grow across the land. His actions still affect our lives more than 2,000 years later!

Life Lesson:
God can use anyone to fulfill His purposes.

Family Activity

Gather all the ingredients you need to bake Christmas cookies and make some! Before cleanup, fill the sink with clean water. From among the supplies and ingredients, select different objects to drop into the water and count the ripples each object makes. Try items of various weights such as a cookie cutter, spoon, chocolate chip, and sprinkle. Is there *anything* that doesn't make a ripple?

It doesn't matter how small the object is, it still has a ripple effect! The same is true in our lives. Every action we take—big or small—affects the people around us. Many small actions often add up to make a huge impact. And like Caesar Augustus, whose actions changed history, we may never know it!

Family Time Questions

- Talk about a time when someone else's actions put you in a good mood.

- How can you pay it forward?

In those days a decree went out from Caesar Augustus that the whole empire should be registered.—Luke 2:1

God, multiply our actions to affect others and bless Your name, even in ways we'll never know.

Bethlehem

Character Trait:
Steadfast

Life Lesson:
Jesus is all we need.

Bethlehem and the Christmas Story

Bethlehem is the small village where Jesus was born. Although not a person, the city itself plays an important role in the Christmas story. Joseph and Mary returned to Bethlehem for the census because it was where Joseph's ancestors had lived. The four- or five-day journey to Bethlehem was about eighty miles of hills and rough terrain, which was hard on Mary because she was about to have her baby. Although the journey was difficult, Mary stayed *steadfast*. That means she kept going and did not give up.

Bethlehem was also a fitting place for Jesus to be born because it means "house of bread." When Jesus grew up, He called Himself the "bread of life" (John 6:35), meaning He gives us all we need for life. Whenever we face hard times, like Mary did on the road to Bethlehem, we can always rely on Jesus to help us keep going. The bread symbolizes how Jesus is steadfast for us. That means He helps us follow God and not give up.

Family Activity

Play a board game that your family enjoys but often takes longer than your kids can sit still for. As they grow weary, encourage your children to finish the game until the end, especially if they get bored. Talk about what it means to be steadfast no matter how we feel. Compare it to Mary's journey to Bethlehem.

Afterward, have bread as a snack. Use butter, jam, or another delicious spread. Make this a special treat. Use the bread as an illustration to teach that Jesus is the Bread of Life. Just like bread gives us the energy to keep going during the day, Jesus will help us not give up in following God, even when it's hard. He will help us be steadfast.

Family Time Questions

- Talk about a recent challenge you had to overcome.

- How did you get through it?

Joseph also went up from the town of Nazareth in Galilee, to Judea, to the city of David, which is called Bethlehem, because he was of the house and family line of David, to be registered along with Mary, who was engaged to him and was pregnant. –Luke 2:4–5

God, help us remain steadfast on our journey, relying on You for everything we need.

The Manger

Character Trait:
Hospitable

The Manger and the Christmas Story

Remember, Joseph and Mary returned to Bethlehem for the census. The custom for ancestors returning to the City of David was to show hospitality, especially for a woman who was pregnant. *Hospitality* is welcoming someone else into your home in a thoughtful way. Sadly, when Joseph and Mary arrived, there was no room for them in the inn. The Greek word *inn* means "guest room," which was likely a house where Joseph's extended family lived. Sadly, the guest room was already full because so many people had come back for the census!

So, out of hospitality, Mary and Joseph were put in a lower room, or main living area of the house. This is also where animals were kept warm at night. While she stayed there, Mary gave birth to Baby Jesus. She wrapped Him in cloths and laid Jesus in a manger, which was a feeding trough for the animals. The manger wasn't anything majestic, but it was a sign of hospitality, and it was where the most hospitable Person ever was laid. Jesus welcomes everyone to trust in Him and enter the kingdom of God! And like the manger, we can prepare our hearts as a place for Jesus to come stay. When Jesus lives in our hearts, we become more like Him, serving others in hospitality.

Life Lesson:
Serve others.

Family Activity

Invite another person or family into your home this week for a meal and to play games. Consider welcoming a widow who lives alone, a family in need of emotional support, or a single parent. Make sure your children invest something in the activity. For example, they can donate one of their toys to a child in need or participate in making a dessert.

Use this activity to help your kids understand the hospitality of the manger scene. Jesus was swaddled and laid where the animals' food went. Then He grew up to become the source of true food (the bread of life) we all need (see Day 11). As a family, continue inviting others who need to be fed with Christ's love and hospitality into your home.

Family Time Questions

- Has God laid someone on your heart who needs hospitality this Christmas? Maybe a friend at school or someone you know at church?

- What is something you can do for that person?

Then she gave birth to her firstborn son, and she wrapped him tightly in cloth and laid him in a manger, because there was no guest room available for them. –Luke 2:7

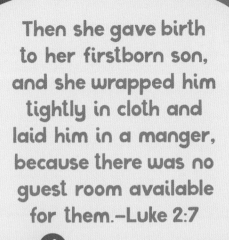

God, show us how to be hospitable and to count others as more significant than ourselves.

Jesus

Character Trait:
Loving

Jesus and the Christmas Story

Jesus *is* the Christmas story! Without Jesus, we would all be in big trouble. We all need a Savior to rescue us from sin. As the angel said, Jesus' arrival is "good news of great joy that will be for all the people" (Luke 2:10). God the Father loved us so much that He chose to send His only Son from heaven to earth to be born as a baby.

But this is not where the good news ends. Jesus loved us so much that He grew up, lived the perfect life, and died in our place to suffer for our sin. Then Jesus came back to life three days later! He went up to heaven and lives there today. Because Jesus is alive, we can have an incredible relationship with God right now and forever. This is the best news of all! When we believe in Jesus, we become children of God. He guides us, makes His home with us, becomes our friend, teaches us His ways, and hears our prayers. Even more, we can love others the way God loves us. Jesus said, "As the Father has loved me, I have also loved you. Remain in my love" (John 15:9). This incredible love is the whole point of Christmas. It is the best news we will ever hear!

Life Lesson:
God loves *you*.

Family Activity

Plan a birthday party for Jesus. You can choose to have the party on Christmas Day or whenever it suits your family plans. Either way, work with your children today to plan the party. Purchase the ingredients to bake a cake. Buy balloons or other decorations. On the day of the party, sing carols and "Happy Birthday." Tell stories of how Jesus changed your life. Make this celebration unique to your family. Create a tradition you can all look forward to every year.

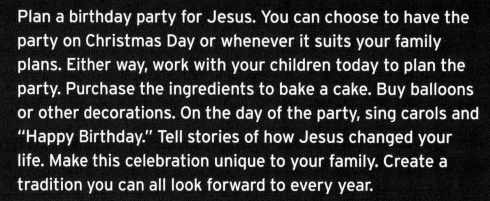

Family Time Questions

- Describe the good news of how much Jesus loves you.

- How does Jesus' love for you change the way you think about Christmas?

- How does it change the way you treat other people? Give examples.

But the angel said to them, "Don't be afraid,
for look, I proclaim to you good news of
great joy that will be for all the people:
Today in the city of David a Savior was born
for you, who is the Messiah, the Lord."
–Luke 2:10–11

*Jesus, thank You for coming into
the world and dying for our sins.
Help us abide in Your love.*

Shepherds

Character Trait: Adoring

The Shepherds and the Christmas Story

Like Mary, the mother of Jesus, the shepherds living in Jesus' day had little razzle-dazzle. They were not highly thought of. Being a shepherd was hard work, and the job was often left to the youngest child in the family. Even David, before he became king, was dismissed when he was just a shepherd boy. Yet God often reveals Himself to the most overlooked people in the world to show that He cares most about what's inside our hearts.

In Luke 2, you can almost hear the excitement in the shepherds' voices as they hurried off to Bethlehem to find Jesus. Seeing Him with their own eyes, they *adored* Jesus, meaning they loved everything about Him. On their way back to the fields, the shepherds couldn't keep silent about what they had seen.

They told everyone they saw how much they adored Him! Years later, during His ministry, Jesus said, "I am the good shepherd. The good shepherd lays down his life for the sheep" (John 10:11). Jesus was talking about dying on the cross to pay the price for our sin. Perhaps that's the very reason God uses these excited shepherds as His first messengers to share the good news about the birth of Jesus!

Life Lesson:
Adore Jesus and tell others about Him.

Family Activity

The prophet Isaiah wrote, "How beautiful on the mountains *are the feet of those who bring good news*, who proclaim peace, who bring good tidings, who proclaim salvation, who say to Zion, 'Your God reigns!'" (Isaiah 52:7 NIV, emphasis added). Imagine the feet of the shepherds that first Christmas running throughout the countryside proclaiming the Good News of Jesus!

Tonight, use your feet to bring the Good News. Begin at home. Together, pray and ask God to increase your adoration for Him. Then go for a family prayer walk around your neighborhood, praying for the people in each house. Use this activity as a springboard for talking to your kids more about how you can share the love of Jesus with those around you.

Family Time Questions

- What is something you adore so much you love telling others about it (a toy, a friend, a memory, etc.)?

- Have you ever told someone about Jesus with that same excitement?

The shepherds said to one another, "Let's go straight to Bethlehem and see what has happened, which the Lord has made known to us." They hurried off and found ... the baby who was lying in the manger.... The shepherds returned, glorifying and praising God.–Luke 2:15–20

God, give us the heart to respond to Your birth the way the shepherds did, with praise and adoration.

Angels

Character
Trait:

Strong

The Angels and the Christmas Story

In the Bible, we often read about angels sending messages to God's people. Remember Gabriel? His messages to Zechariah and to Mary sparked the Christmas story as we know it. Besides Gabriel, Michael is the only other angel whose name we know. But many more exist! The Bible tells us millions upon millions of angels worship God, serve Him, and carry out His instructions. Sometimes you might meet an angel without knowing it (Hebrews 13:2)!

However, angels aren't necessarily the sweet, gentle, winged beings we often see portrayed in nativity scenes. The Bible describes angels as having "great strength" and obeying God (Psalm 103:20). Perhaps that's why, when the shepherds saw the angel in the field surrounded by the glory of God, they were terrified. Yet the angel said, "Don't be afraid" (Luke 2:10). Then, all of sudden, many more angels lit up the night skies above the shepherds as the first messengers to proclaim the birth of the Savior to the world. Coming in strength, the angels delivered a message unlike any other: The light of the whole world—God's Son, Jesus—had come! His power would defeat the darkness of sin, once and for all.

Life Lesson: Walk in the light.

Family Activity

Not only did the angels praise God, but they lit up the night sky above the shepherds. They proclaimed victory over the dark forces of evil with the birth of the promised Messiah.

Tonight, everyone put on Christmas pajamas. Pop some popcorn. Pile into your car. Drive around eating popcorn and looking at the decorated houses lighting up the night sky in and around your neighborhood. Talk about how the bright Christmas lights have the strength to pierce the darkness and light up the houses. In a similar way, when we follow Jesus, who is the "light of the world," we have the strength to "never walk in the darkness" because we "have the light of life" shining inside of us (John 8:12).

Family Time Questions

- What do you think it means to "walk in the light"?

- Why do you think we need to pray for strength to do so?

Suddenly there was a multitude of the heavenly host with the angel, praising God and saying: "Glory to God in the highest heaven, and peace on earth to people he favors!"–Luke 2:13–14

Father, send Your angels to minister to and protect our family so we can walk strongly in the light.

Simeon

Character Trait:
Listening

Simeon and the Christmas Story

Simeon's name means "hearing." True to his name, Simeon listened for God's voice. He paid close attention to live according to what the Scriptures taught. Simeon wanted both to hear from God and to see Him, so he prayed a lot. One day, he heard the Holy Spirit tell him that he would not die until he saw Jesus in real life. Imagine that!

Simeon was well along in age when his part of the Christmas story began. Led by the Holy Spirit, he went to the temple the same day that Mary and Joseph came to dedicate Jesus. While Jesus looked like every other baby at the temple, Simeon knew—by listening to the Holy Spirit—that Jesus was the one and only Messiah. When he saw Mary and Joseph, Simeon joyously picked Baby Jesus up in his arms and praised God. God blessed Simeon for his faith. Simeon had desired to see God his whole life. And because Simeon listened, he was one of the first to hold Baby Jesus and to understand that Jesus was God in the flesh.

Life Lesson: Seek God and hear from Him.

Family Activity

Simeon held Baby Jesus in his arms! Though we won't get to hold Jesus in our arms, we can hold Him in our hearts.

Find a doll. Invite each person to role play the scene of Simeon first laying his eyes on Baby Jesus. Imagine what Simeon felt when he got to hold Baby Jesus after praying for so many years. Hold the doll the way you think Simeon may have. When it's your turn to hold the baby, share what Jesus means to you. Help your kids think through this by asking them questions like, "If you could shout from the roof what you love about Jesus, what would you say? What makes you grateful for Jesus? How has Jesus changed you?"

Family Time Questions

- What is one way you want to begin seeking Jesus with more of your heart?

- What is one way you hear from God?

Simeon took him up in his arms, praised God, and said, "Now, Master, you can dismiss your servant in peace, as you promised. For my eyes have seen your salvation."–Luke 2:28–30

Dear God, like Simeon, give us the desire to hear Your voice and follow it. Show us the way to salvation in Jesus.

Anna

Character
Trait:
Patient

Anna and the Christmas Story

Anna, like Simeon, was of old age when her part in the Christmas story began. Many years before, she had been widowed after only seven years of marriage. Can you imagine the heartache as a young bride? Though she could have turned her back on God, Anna chose to seek God and godly community instead. The Bible says she worshiped God at the temple, spending her days and nights there. Anna, like Simeon, waited patiently on God's arrival into the world, even in her distress.

The word *wait* in the Bible is a verb. In Luke 2:25 (NIV), the Greek word for *wait* means "to look forward to" or "to expect." In this instance, the word means that both Simeon and Anna expected the first Advent. They knew, without a doubt, that Jesus was coming, but they had no idea when! Because Anna spent her entire life serving God, she was in the temple on the same day as Simeon. Having a close relationship with God, she also recognized Mary and Joseph when they entered the temple with Jesus. The Bible tells us that when Anna saw Baby Jesus, she blessed Him and began telling everyone about Him. Her wait was worth it!

Life Lesson: Waiting on God is worth it.

Family Activity

Use crayons and construction paper. Everyone draws a picture of "Poor Waiting," or a time you did not wait well. Tell your family the story about your picture. How did not waiting well make you feel? How did it make others around you feel? Then everyone draws another picture of "Expectant Waiting," or ways you can honor God while you wait. Talk about ways you can wait on God with faith, without being bummed out, and with gratitude and expectation of what God will do. How does waiting in this way make you and everyone around you feel?

Family Time Questions

- Is there a prayer of yours God hasn't answered yet?

- What might be some reasons God makes us wait on Him?

There was also a prophetess, Anna,
a daughter of Phanuel, of the tribe of Asher....
She did not leave the temple, serving God night
and day with fasting and prayers. —Luke 2:36–37

God, even when we don't like
it, help us wait on You. Give us
a desire to serve You all of our
days, just like Anna.

King Herod

Character
Trait:
Jealous

King Herod and the Christmas Story

King Herod is the villain of the Christmas story. He was the cruel ruler over the Jews leading up to the birth of Jesus. When he found out that Jesus, "the King of the Jews," had been born, he became jealous. Herod wanted to be the only king. He could not stand the thought of sharing his power or, worse, losing it. King Herod told the wise men—who had traveled a long way to see Jesus—to come back and tell him when they found the baby so that he, too, could worship Jesus. But Herod was lying. He wanted to kill Baby Jesus! Later, when King Herod learned that the wise men tricked him and did not return, he went into a fit of rage.

King Herod did not like that someone else had something he had—the title of king. He grew so jealous that he came up with an evil plot to have Jesus killed, ordering that every boy two years old and under in and around Bethlehem be put to death. King Herod's jealousy drove him crazy and led him to make evil choices.

When you love a position, person, or possession more than you love Jesus, you will become jealous at the thought of losing it. This is why the Bible teaches us to be content by loving the Giver—God Himself—more than what He gives us.

Life Lesson:
Practice being content.

Family Activity

Set up a family activity to teach what jealousy feels like. If you have multiple children, you could distribute toys in uneven ways, giving one child an iPad, one child an old book, and one child a toy. For only children, you might play a video game while your child is assigned a chore. Observe their behavior. After a few minutes, ask your kids how they feel. Who is whining? Is anybody in a fit of rage? Did anyone try to take another's toy? Talk about jealousy and connect the activity with what King Herod was feeling. Brainstorm with your kids how they can practice being content when they feel jealous toward another person.

✳ Family Time Questions

- Talk about a time when you felt jealous.

- What can you do the next time this feeling comes?

- How can you be content, or happier, with what you have?

When King Herod heard this, he was deeply disturbed, and all Jerusalem with him. So he assembled all the chief priests and scribes of the people and asked them where the Messiah would be born. –Matthew 2:3–4

God, make our hearts content. Thank You for all the ways You continue to provide for us.

The Star

★

Character
Trait:
Discerning

The Star and the Christmas Story

The Star of Bethlehem was a sign to the wise men, or *magi*, that Jesus had come. The magi lived in the east and were smart. They had studied the stars and planets for years. They knew that a unique star appearing in the sky meant the Messiah from the ancient prophecy would be born. The star was so unique that nobody else seemed to notice it. But the magi were *discerning*. This means they paid careful attention to how God was leading them and what He was saying through Scripture.

Knowing the star's significance, the magi left their homes and followed it, hoping to find the Messiah. The star led them all the way to Jerusalem. When they arrived unexpectedly, they asked King Herod where the King of the Jews was living. King Herod sent them to Bethlehem, and on their way, the star reappeared. Seeing it again overwhelmed them with joy!

Because the earth rotates on its axis, stars appear to be slowly moving above us. But the Star of Bethlehem did not move. It stopped above the place Jesus was, proving that it was most likely a supernatural event, just like Jesus' birth. While the wise men could not explain this miracle, they trusted God's Word and followed His leading.

Life Lesson:
When God leads, we follow.

Family Activity

Go outside on a clear night to study the stars and look for the constellations. Breathe in the Christmas air. Discuss what the magi might have been feeling as they walked at night, trying to follow the Star of Bethlehem. Think about their journey—the fear of Herod, the excitement of seeing Jesus, the exhaustion from their travels, and even the fear of robbers.

Back inside, ask everyone to write about or draw a picture of what it feels like to follow Jesus. Ask, "What emotion do you feel right now on *your* journey? Excitement about where He's leading you? Fear that God might have left you?" Put the Star of Bethlehem at the top of your pictures as a reminder to keep following Him. God always carries out His promises.

Family Time Questions

- How does God speak to us today?

- Have you ever done something you thought God was leading you to do?

After hearing the king, they went on their way. And there it was—the star they had seen at its rising. It led them until it came and stopped above the place where the child was. When they saw the star, they were overwhelmed with joy.—Matthew 2:9–10

God, overwhelm us with joy as You lead us. Teach us to follow You and to trust in Your promises.

Magi

Character Trait:
Generous

The Magi and the Christmas Story

The *magi*, also known as wise men, traveled from the east to find Jesus. Many Bible teachers believe these men studied the science of space, or what we call *astronomy* today. They believe the magi were smart, wealthy, and highly respected men. While the Bible doesn't tell us how many magi journeyed to see Jesus, the traditional teaching is three. That's because they brought Him three generous gifts of gold, frankincense, and myrrh.

Bible teachers say the magi did not arrive at Jesus' house until He was between sixteen and twenty-four months old. When they entered the house and laid eyes on Jesus, they fell to their knees, presented their gifts, and worshiped Him. Then God warned them in a dream not to tell King Herod where Jesus was since God knew Herod wanted to kill Jesus (see Day 18). Obeying God, they returned to their home in the east a different way.

The magi were the very first *Gentiles*, or non-Jewish people, mentioned in the Bible to worship Jesus as the Messiah. They understood the significance of Jesus' birth. God Himself had come to earth as a man—what a generous gift from heaven! They responded by giving back to Him in a generous way.

Life Lesson: Be generous.

Family Activity

For this activity, be generous as a family. Invite your children to give away a toy or use their own money to buy a present for a family in need. Deliver the gift with your child. Or lead your children to give their own money in the church offering. Together, consider other ways you can be generous and give extra as a family. Use this activity to discuss how Jesus' love for us is a gift and how one way to give back to Him is by being generous toward others.

Family Time Questions

- What is a favorite gift you have given someone?
* How did giving it away make you feel?

Entering the house, they saw the child with Mary his mother, and falling to their knees, they worshiped him.—Matthew 2:11

Heavenly Father, help us give generously as a way to worship You.

Gold

Character Trait:
Honoring

Gold and the Christmas Story

Gold is a highly treasured metal and one of the gifts the magi brought to Jesus. Though we don't know how much gold the magi gave, wise Bible teachers believe gold was worth more during Jesus' time than it is today. So even a small quantity could have helped Mary and Joseph take care of Jesus!

The gift of gold was used in Bible times to honor a king. *Honoring* others means showing them respect. We can do this by giving gifts, sharing meaningful words, or acting in thoughtful ways. The magi knew Baby Jesus was not an ordinary baby. He is the "KING OF KINGS" and the "LORD OF LORDS" (Revelation 19:16). While the magi were honorable men, they understood that Jesus deserved more honor than they did—even as a toddler! Their gift of gold honored Jesus as the King of kings.

While many kings and world leaders make bad decisions because of sin, Jesus is the perfect King and the ruler over all the kings of the earth. His throne is built on righteousness and justice, and His kingdom never ends.

Life Lesson:
Jesus is the King of kings.

Family Activity

Sit down together and make honor lists. Everyone creates a list of three to five things to admire about everyone else in your family. Use construction paper, markers, crayons, magazines, newspapers, and more to make these lists. Then take the time to honor each person aloud. Post your honor lists where everyone in your family can see them. If there are multiple children in your family, help them use the list as inspiration to find more creative ways to honor their siblings.

Family Time Questions

- If you had the power to make one rule everyone had to follow, what rule would you make?

- How does that rule bring honor to others?

Then they opened their
treasures and presented him
with gifts: gold, frankincense,
and myrrh.–Matthew 2:11

*Father, help us
honor You as our
King. You are the
King of kings!*

Frankincense

Character
Trait:

Confessing

Frankincense and the Christmas Story

Frankincense is the second gift the magi gave Jesus. Like gold, frankincense was also quite expensive when Jesus lived. It was an *incense*, or perfume, that priests commonly burned in worship to God. *Priests* were men who came to God on behalf of the people.

Just as the gift of gold showed that Jesus was King, the gift of frankincense meant that Jesus was a priest. Known as our Great High Priest, Jesus' priesthood means we can talk directly to God! We also don't have to practice special routines when we sin like people had to do in the Old Testament. Instead, we just have to confess our sin to Jesus in prayer.

Jesus is our *intercessor*, which means He takes our prayers to God for us. The Bible uses incense to describe the prayers of believers. Confessing our sins to God in prayer is like an aroma, or a nice smell, that is pleasing to Him.

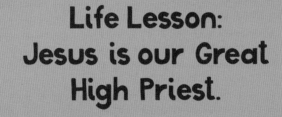

Life Lesson:
Jesus is our Great High Priest.

Family Activity

Teach your kids the five-finger prayer to help them focus on specific things when they pray. Since your thumb is the closest finger to your body, use it to pray for the people closest to you, such as parents, siblings, grandparents, and friends. Next, use your pointer finger to pray for teachers, pastors, or coaches. The middle finger is the biggest finger, so it reminds us to give thanks to our big God. Then, use your ring finger to pray for the sick or those in need. Finally, the pinkie finger leads us to pray for our own needs and confess our sins. Simplify or adjust this activity based on your children's age and understanding.

Family Time Questions

- Is there someone you know who is especially hurting right now? How do you want to pray for that person?

* What sins do you want to confess to Jesus, our Great High Priest?

Then they opened their treasures and presented him with gifts: gold, frankincense, and myrrh.–Matthew 2:11

Lord Jesus, forgive us of our sin. May our confession be a pleasing aroma to You.

Myrrh

Character
Trait:
Sacrificial

Myrrh and the Christmas Story

Myrrh is the third gift the magi gave Jesus. Similar to frankincense, it has a pleasing smell. However, in Bible times, myrrh was connected to suffering and used as an embalming oil when a person died.

The meaning of this gift was not recognized at the moment by the rest of the world. It pointed to Jesus' future death as a sacrifice for our sins. Many prophecies throughout the Old Testament warned of Jesus' pain and suffering, and myrrh was an important part of His story. For example, when it was time for Jesus to die on the cross, the soldiers offered wine mixed with myrrh to ease the pain. But Jesus refused it. Then after Jesus' death, Nicodemus brought myrrh to use during Jesus' burial.

Jesus' love is *sacrificial*. That means He loves you so much He gave up His own life so you can live. Myrrh is a symbol of Jesus' sacrifice. By His sacrificial love, Jesus modeled for us how to "carry one another's burdens," even when it feels difficult (Galatians 6:2).

Life Lesson: Carry one another's burdens.

Family Activity

Invite your children to grab some coins. In private, put a five-dollar bill up your sleeve. Tell your kids if they sacrifice their change by handing it over to you, they may never see it again, but for a good reason. If they choose to surrender it, give them the five-dollar bill you had up your sleeve. If they don't, show them what they missed.

Tell a story of how a sacrifice in your life brought you unexpected joy, patience, faith, or a closer relationship with Jesus. As a family, share what sacrifices you have made at school, at work, on teams, at church, for mission work, and more.

Family Time Questions

- Has anyone ever sacrificed something for you?

- Have you sacrificed something for someone else?

* How can you carry somebody else's burden?

Then they opened their treasures and presented him with gifts: gold, frankincense, and myrrh.—Matthew 2:11

God, thank You for giving up Your life for us. Teach us to carry the burdens of others even when it feels difficult.

Egypt

Character Trait:
Safe

Egypt and the Christmas Story

Egypt is where Joseph and Mary took Jesus to protect Him from King Herod. Remember that King Herod was planning to kill all the boys in his kingdom who were two years old and under (see Day 18). Imagine how Joseph and Mary felt. They had to leave everything that was comfortable to them and travel to Egypt, a foreign land. But God knew Egypt was a safe place, so He sent them there to protect Jesus. Joseph and Mary raised Jesus there until King Herod died not much later.

As a young boy, Jesus was a refugee living in a foreign land. A *refugee* is someone who lives in another country instead of their homeland. Do you know who else are refugees? We are! The Bible calls those who believe in Jesus "foreigners and temporary residents," or *spiritual refugees*, on earth (Hebrews 11:13). We don't belong in a sinful world. Our real home is with God, living on a new earth without sin. The Bible describes this new earth like the original garden of Eden, without sin, sickness, or heartache.

Jesus promised to prepare a place for us in our true home. The Bible also promises that God can be our *refuge*, or safe place, today when we put our trust in Him!

Life Lesson:
God is our true refuge.

Family Activity

Take some time to study current refugee situations around the world. Do this ahead of time so you can explain what a *refugee* is in a child-friendly way. Talk to your kids about how seeing ourselves as spiritual refugees helps us relate to those, just like Jesus, who need to flee their homes for safety. Take time to pray for children who live in unsafe situations. Ask Jesus to be their refuge and strength this Christmas.

If your family sponsors children in other parts of the world, write them a letter or send them a Christmas gift.

Family Time Questions

- Talk about a time when you found safety in God.

- What do you think it would feel like to be a refugee today?

- How can we pray for refugees today?

After they were gone, an angel of the Lord appeared to Joseph in a dream, saying, "Get up! Take the child and his mother, flee to Egypt, and stay there until I tell you."—Matthew 2:13

Heavenly Father, You are our refuge when we need You. Teach us to be a safe place for others in need.

Nazareth

Character Trait:
Understanding

Life Lesson:
Jesus understands our circumstances.

Nazareth and the Christmas Story

After King Herod died, an angel told Joseph to take Mary and Jesus back to Israel. Jesus grew up in a town called Nazareth and lived there until He began His public ministry at age thirty. In Nazareth, Jesus learned to be a carpenter, or a craftsman, from His dad, Joseph.

When Jesus began His ministry in Nazareth, the people in His community grew so angry that they wanted to disown Him. Because of this, Jesus moved to Capernaum and didn't perform miracles in Nazareth. Like Mary, the shepherds, and so many other parts of the Christmas story, *Nazarenes*, or people from Nazareth, were thought of as unimportant. They were not well liked. Hearing that Jesus was a Nazarene, one of His future disciples asked, "Can anything good come out of Nazareth?" (John 1:46).

Even though Jesus came from heaven, He entered this world in an unimpressive way. As a baby, He slept in a manger. As a child, He lived as a refugee. As a teenager, He learned carpentry in Nazareth. As an adult, Jesus "didn't have an impressive form or majesty that we should look at him" (Isaiah 53:2). Why did Jesus live like this? Jesus chose to live a humble life so that He could relate to us. Now we can confidently know that Jesus understands everything we experience. Jesus is our humble King!

Family Activity

Merry Christmas! Happy birthday, Jesus! Keep it simple with your activity today. Choose one of the following:

- *Everyone shares a favorite day from this Advent family experience.* Draw a picture that explains why you loved that day so much. Write that day's character trait at the top of the page and hang it where you can practice it in the coming months.

- *Everyone chooses one character trait or life lesson to focus on next year.* Write the word or phrase down and hang it in your room. Ask the other members of your family to help you grow.

Family Time Questions

- Is there anything that confuses you about the Christmas story?

- What is the most important lesson you learned this Christmas?

Then [Joseph] went and settled in a
town called Nazareth to fulfill what
was spoken through the prophets, that
[Jesus] would be called a Nazarene.
–Matthew 2:23

*Dear God, thank You for the
Christmas story! We love You
and worship You today.*

Christmas Memories

As parents with young kids, we often find ourselves rushing bedtime or bouncing from one task to the next, especially during the busy days of December. We may have a beautiful moment with one child but forget about it a minute later because another child is in tears and demanding our attention. Exasperated, we forget the silly comments and sweet parenting moments God gifts to us.

That is why we created a memory section in this book. Our most powerful memories form in the context of relational experiences and shared emotions: the gut-wrenching belly laughs over a funny incident, the heartbreaking tears after losing a beloved pet, or the sheer joy of a spontaneous dance party after putting on Christmas pajamas. These memories form the foundation of our future relationships with family.

Our prayer is that during this Advent family experience, you make many memories to cherish and pass on for years to come. This section provides plenty of space to record your children's answers to the Family Time Questions and the fun memories you share during the Family Activities.

Don't forget to record details about the experience, such as your child's age, the date, and any context to help you remember the moment. We hope this book becomes a keepsake for your family, not only as a means to remember shared moments but also as a reminder of how God showed up for your family in big ways in the early years.

Merry Christmas!